Joggin' Your Noggin

With Memorable Events
1920-1970

Mary Randolph, MS
Speech-Language Pathologist

ISBN -13: 978-1511763981
ISBN: -10: 1511763981

DEDICATION

To my amazing mother, Helen, whose incredibly positive attitude inspired me to write books for individuals, like her, confronting dementia. Mom taught us to face every challenge with courage and conviction; to appreciate differences; to be grateful for blessings; to strive to make a difference; and to recognize the value of each new day. Although Alzheimer's quickly reduced her short term memory and gradually diminished her reading and thinking skills, Mom continued to experience so much joy in simply sharing small moments.

Also to readers and their loved ones who continue to enjoy precious times, whether engaging in the present or reminiscing about the past.

INTRODUCTION

A book that highlights significant world events over the fifty-year period from 1920-1970, this "Joggin' Your Noggin" aims to bring entertainment and mental stimulation to readers. Reflecting on the past can be a source of joy, not only for those with dementia, but for many others, especially as they approach their "golden years." Milestones include historical, technological, scientific and cultural happenings related to inventions, politics, songs, famous musicians, TV/movie stars, food, fashion and more. Information is presented in a "fill-in-the-blank" format, with straightforward answers conveniently provided on the reverse of each page. The objective, however, is not to arrive at a correct response, but rather to recall the past and perhaps reawaken a fond memory.

Remembering the "good old days" can be fun and oftentimes conjures up delightful thoughts and feelings. In some instances, seniors will read the book independently. Since each description ends with a blank, the reader is given a chance to "jog" their "noggin" and identify the missing word(s). But the more important benefit is simply to think back and enjoy "warm and fuzzy" feelings. Connecting an event with a memorable personal experience may evoke positive emotions. The book offers countless opportunities to reflect, reminisce and hopefully relive moments of joy.

For example, the first home game at Yankee Stadium was played between the Yankees and the Red Sox in 1923. If reading the book with your father, you might ask questions like, "Did you ever go to Yankee Stadium? Who played and won? How did you get there? Who went with you?" Try to evoke the sounds of the crowd, the smell of the food, the comfort of the seating. You might expand further by singing, "Take Me Out to the Ballgame" or talking about your dad playing baseball or other favorite sports. The more you can relive personal experiences, with all of their associated sights, sounds, smells, tastes and feelings, the better!

If reading the book with your mother, you might reflect on the introduction of sliced bread in 1928. You can talk about favorite kinds of sandwiches or the family's favorite bakery or deli. Recall holidays when your mom baked home-made bread: how she activated yeast, kneaded dough, tested for "doneness" and smeared butter on the first warm slice. Perhaps Mom had a favorite kind of bread -- plain white "Wonder" bread, "Pepperidge Farm" raisin or Jewish rye with caraway seeds. The object is to enjoy the interaction and conversation!

Seniors may also enjoy group discussions of historical milestones and sharing fond memories. Activities Directors in senior centers, assisted living facilities or nursing homes may find "Joggin" a useful resource when creating entertaining games.

Content was gleaned from a variety of sources, including internet sites and historical texts. In some instances, inconsistencies were noted and accuracy of the information could not be ascertained. The author respectfully requests that she not be held accountable. In such cases, the reader is asked to "take it with a grain of salt." The inadvertent inclusion of any "fake news" will hopefully not detract from the enjoyment of reading, reminiscing and sharing.

PLEASE NOTE: You will find more examples and tips to help relive moments of joy throughout the book. Further discussion will be provided at the start of each decade in the section entitled "Let's Preview."

LET'S PREVIEW THE 20s

At the end of World War I, Americans wanted to enjoy a better, simpler, happier life. This decade was known as the "Roaring Twenties" and the "Jazz Age," a time in which women gained the vote, Native Americans became citizens, and people enjoyed speakeasies and dancing the Charleston, notwithstanding prohibition. This was also a time for invention: in science, transportation, and communication. Television, insulin, the electrocardiogram, penicillin, the Model "A" Ford--all made headlines. New sports venues sprang up: Wimbledon, Yankee Stadium and the Rose Bowl; and stars like Charlie Chaplin, Lon Cheney and Laurel and Hardy brought endless entertainment. On the political front, Nazi power grew, the Farm Labor Party and League of Nations formed, and Hoover was appointed Director of the FBI.

Many readers will recall parents' or grandparents' discussions of their favorite form of entertainment. Did they ever go to the Cotton Club or a "speakeasy?" What kind of music was played in their home? Consider your personal preferences for music and dance. Do you have a favorite song or singer? Did you ever attend or participate in concerts or musicals? Whom did you see? Where was the performance? What did you wear? Did you enjoy music in school, ever play a musical instrument or take voice lessons? Once again, try to embellish the memory with as many sights, sounds and feelings as possible. Of course these questions might easily lead to singing or getting up and dancing—all will add to the positive moment.

Remember, the objective is to enjoy your recollections. Let your thoughts wander--stream of consciousness is fine. Don't try to stick to one topic; just "go with the flow." And if reading with a friend, companion or caregiver, appreciate the fact that individuals remember events differently, so don't worry about the accuracy of memories!

1920

1. Hamilton Beach Company introduced the first hand-held hair _____.
2. Alcoholic beverages became illegal, beginning the "dry" period of _____.
3. On August 18th Congress passed the 19th Amendment, granting women the right to _____.
4. The bars or clubs that illegally sold alcohol during Prohibition were called "_____."
5. Chocolate covered ice cream on a stick was introduced in Ohio and called the "Good _____."
6. Eugene O'Neill won the Pulitzer Prize for "Beyond the _____."
7. The Farmer Labor Party was organized in this Illinois city: _____.
8. The New York Yankees signed this remarkable player for $100,000: _____.
9. The League of Nations held its first meeting in Geneva, _____.
10. Children's author Johnny Gruelle introduced Raggedy Ann's brother, Raggedy _____.

Answers to 1920

1... Dryer
2... Prohibition
3... Vote
4... Speakeasies
5... Humor Bar
6... Horizon
7... Chicago
8... Babe Ruth
9... Switzerland
10... Andy

1921

1. The popular breakfast cereal known as "the breakfast of champions" was called "_____."
2. California beat Ohio State 28-0 in this annual January first football competition in L.A.: The Rose _____.
3. The full-length silent film, "The Kid," was released, starring Jackie Coogan and Charlie _____.
4. A major league baseball team purchased 20 acres in Bronx, NY, to build _____.
5. A fictional lady became key in Gold Medal Flour's advertising of foods and recipes, Betty _____.
6. The National Socialist German Workers (Nazi) Party named its new leader, _____.
7. A professional baseball game was broadcast for the first time on _____.
8. The first Miss America Beauty Pageant was held in _____.
9. President Warren G. Harding dedicated the Tomb of The Unknown Soldier in Washington, D.C.'s _____.
10. May 3rd marked the birth of famous prize fighter Sugar Ray_____.

Answers to 1921

1... Wheaties
2... Bowl
3... Chaplin
4... Yankee Stadium
5... Crocker
6... Adolf Hitler
7... Radio
8... Atlantic City
9... Arlington National
   Cemetery
10... Robinson

TENNIS

1922

1. Young women in the 20s who wore short dresses, bobbed hair and makeup were known as "_____."
2. A 99-foot-tall memorial was dedicated in Washington, D.C. to honor a former president, _____.
3. A new concrete tennis stadium was created in London, England and called _____.
4. A newly developed drug, insulin, was used to treat _____.
5. The famous Tomb of Tutankhamen was discovered in the Valley of the Kings in _____.
6. One of the best-selling US magazines, known for its condensed articles and stories, was called "Reader's _____."
7. A private company to broadcast radio services in the UK was created and known as the _____.
8. "The Meaning of Relativity" was released by Albert _____.
9. On August 4th, telephones were silenced for one minute to honor the passing of Alexander _____.
10. June 10th marked the birth of Judy Garland, screen star of the movie "The Wizard of _____."

Answers to 1922

1... Flappers
2... Abraham Lincoln
3... Wimbledon
4... Diabetes
5... Egypt
6... Digest
7... British Broadcasting
    Company
8... Einstein
9... Graham Bell
10... Oz

1923

1. This 4-person game, long popular in China, played with ivory tiles engraved with Chinese characters was called _____.

2. Ethyl gasoline was first marketed in Dayton, _____.

3. Children were thrilled to play with engines, extra cars, tracks and signals with their _____.

4. The US Attorney General declared it legal for women to wear this article of clothing anywhere: _____.

5. This famous magician removed a straight-jacket while suspended 40 feet above ground: Harry _____.

6. A popular comic strip featured would-be prize fighter Moon _____.

7. The "Hollywood" sign was officially dedicated in the hills above L.A. and originally read, "_____."

8. The first issue of a weekly news magazine was published and known as "_____."

9. The first home game was played at Yankee Stadium between the New York Yankees and the Boston _____.

10. Actor Lon Cheney gained acclaim as Quasimodo in the film "The Hunchback of _____."

Answers to 1923

1... Mah Jong
2... Ohio
3... Lionel Train Sets
4... Slacks
5... Houdini
6... Mullins
7... Hollywoodland
8... Time
9... Red Sox
10... Notre Dame

1924

1. J. Edgar Hoover was appointed Director of the

   _____.
2. Athletes from around the world headed to France for the first Winter _____.
3. A Massachusetts pie company became known for its tasty 4-inch snack pies, "Table _____."
4. President Coolidge signed the Indian Citizenship Act to grant Native Americans _____.
5. Willem Einthoven won a Nobel Prize for an improved instrument to measure the heart, the _____.
6. Thursday, November 27th marked New York City's first Macy's _____.
7. The fashion industry suddenly exposed arms and legs with the introduction of shocking new _____.
8. Rand McNally published its first road _____.
9. A word-game mania hit the US when Simon and Shuster published the first book of _____.
10. Women began removing their makeup with disposable paper tissues made by _____.

Answers to 1924

1... FBI
2... Olympics
3... Talk
4... Citizenship
5... Electrocardiogram
6... Thanksgiving Day Parade
7... Swimsuits
8... Atlas
9... Crossword Puzzles
10... Kleenex

1925

1. F. Scott Fitzgerald published his novel highlighting life in the 1920s entitled "The Great _____."
2. A South Dakota site was dedicated to honor 4 presidents by carving their faces in stone, Mount _____.
3. In the Scopes Monkey Trial a teacher was charged with violating the law by teaching about _____.
4. After nearly 40 years of catalog sales, this store opened a retail operation in Chicago: _____.
5. The first motel in the US opened, at $1.25 per night, in San Luis Obispo, _____.
6. Adolf Hitler published his personal manifesto known as "Mein _____."
7. The longest-running radio broadcast in the US began in Nashville, and became known as the "Grand _____."
8. Richard G. Drew invented an adhesive tape known as "_____."
9. October 23rd marked the birth of late-night TV star Johnny _____.
10. Lively dancers kicked their legs, turned in their toes and swung their arms when doing the _____.

Answers to 1925

1... Gatsby
2... Rushmore
3... Evolution
4... Sears Roebuck
5... California
6... Kampf
7... Ole Opry
8... Scotch Tape
9... Carson
10... Charleston

1926

1. John Logie Baird created a system to transmit moving images via airwaves called the _____.
2. Spain appointed the youngest general in European history, Francisco _____.
3. The first transatlantic telephone call took place, from London to _____.
4. Aviators Richard Byrd and Floyd Bennet made the first flight over the North _____.
5. This song by Gene Austin hit Number One: "Five Foot Two, Eyes of _____."
6. Young white audiences flocked to hear the latest jazz sounds at Harlem's Cotton _____.
7. The Hormel Company in Minnesota introduced the first canned _____.
8. One of the most destructive storms ever, with strong winds and high storm surges, hit Florida's city of _____.
9. This book known for car valuation was first published: "The Kelley _____."
10. One of Hollywood's all-time sex symbols was born, Marilyn _____.

Answers to 1926

1... Television
2... Franco
3... New York
4... Pole
5... Blue
6... Club
7... Ham
8... Miami
9... Blue Book
10... Monroe

1927

1. The Holland Tunnel connected lower Manhattan in New York City to _____.
2. Charles Lindberg completed the first transatlantic flight direct from New York City to Paris in a plane he called "The Spirit of _____."
3. The Model A car, which reportedly sold over 400,000 in the first two weeks, was released by _____.
4. The first sound motion picture, "The Jazz Singer," opened and starred Al _____.
5. This Broadway musical told the story of a theatrical troupe traveling the Mississippi on a riverboat: "_____."
6. Floods inundated farmlands and killed hundreds during the great flood of this river: _____.
7. A new medicine appeared to relieve nausea heartburn, and indigestion, "Pepto _____."
8. The hand-cranked washing machine was replaced by the _____.
9. A $2.29 price tag was on the "Kodak Box _____."
10. After toasters burned too much bread, Charles Strite invented the first automatic _____.

Answers to 1927

1... Jersey City
2... St. Louis
3... Ford
4... Jolson
5... Show Boat
6... The Mississippi
7... Bismol
8... Electric Washing Machine
9... Brownie Camera
10... Pop-Up Toaster

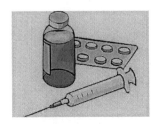

1928

1. This rodent character with big ears made his debut in one of the first animated cartoons with a sound track: _____.

2. Guy Lombardo and his band first played this song as a New Year's Eve song: "Auld Lang _____."

3. Amelia Earhart was the first woman passenger to fly across the _____.

4. Alexander Fleming introduced the age of antibiotics through his discovery of _____.

5. This negative pressure ventilator was first used in the US to help patients breathe: the "iron _____."

6. This hilarious slapstick comedy duo made their film debut: Stan Laurel and Oliver _____.

7. This early rock and roll star was born and later sang his hit song "Blueberry Hill": Fats _____.

8. This D.H. Lawrence novel about an illicit relationship was banned in the UK and US: "Lady _____."

9. A baking company in Missouri sold this product for the first time: sliced _____.

10. A new, stretchy chewing gum recipe was discovered and eventually named "Dubble _____."

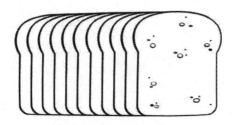

Answers to 1928

1... Mickey Mouse
2... Syne
3... Atlantic
4... Penicillin
5... Lung
6... Hardy
7... Domino
8... Chatterley's Lover
9... Bread
10... Bubble

1929

1. January 15th marked the birth of the most famous leader of the Civil Rights Movement, Martin _____.
2. On October 29th the stock-market crash on Wall Street started the period of the "Great _____."
3. On February 14th seven gangsters were gunned down by Al Capone's men in the crime called "The_____."
4. This NYC museum was founded to exhibit collections of contemporary art: _____.
5. This famous Catholic nun and missionary arrived in India: Mother _____.
6. The motion picture industry presented Emil Jannings and Janet Gaynor with the first Academy _____.
7. A famous comic character, a spinach-eating sailor, made his appearance, _____.
8. The Acadia National Park was established in the Northern New England state of _____.
9. This German-built airship circled the world in 21 days and landed in New Jersey: _____.
10. Motorola made the first car _____.

Answers to 1929

1... Luther King Jr.
2... Depression
3... St. Valentine's Day Massacre
4... MoMA (Museum of Modern Art)
5... Teresa
6... Awards
7... Popeye
8... Maine
9... Zeppelin
10... Radio

LET'S PREVIEW THE 30s

The decade of the 30s was a challenging time. Events like the Great Depression, dust storms over farmlands and an increase in crime posed significant challenge to many Americans. President Roosevelt and the federal government introduced laws and programs to help rebuild the economy. But citizens were forced to find ways to deal with hardship and stay strong during the slow recovery. Fortunately people were able to escape problems through leisure activity: going to the movies, marathon dancing, or playing pinball, "Bingo" or "Monopoly." Progress was celebrated with the opening of the Empire State Building, George Washington and Golden Gate Bridges, and Radio City Music Hall. Despite their worries, citizens sensed pride and joy when listening to the newly-named national anthem, the "Star Spangled Banner."

Thoughts about the Depression might easily lead to memories of your family's financial history. Increase your enjoyment of the book by allowing yourself to reflect on, or have conversation about, related topics. For example, you may recall elderly relatives' stories of struggles to find jobs or depletion of accumulated wealth. Perhaps a parent was forced to drop out of school to help support the family? Or maybe a loved one worked in a government program like the "Civilian Conservation Corps?"

Think about your own employment history. Remember your feelings of pride when you got your first job, promotion or pay raise, or completed an apprenticeship or degree. On the other hand, you may recall worrying, getting little sleep, taking only brief vacations, or needing to defer non-essential purchases when unemployed.

People who struggled financially during the depression often suffered long-lasting effects of that experience. How did your parents continue to spend and save money in later years? Were they more likely to offer financial advice to their children? How did they feel about gambling, contributing to charity or volunteering their services? What, if anything, did they learn about the true source of happiness?

Enjoy the opportunity to reflect on your life's experiences and share them with others. Don't worry about sticking to one topic. And remember, don't judge the truth or accuracy of recollections—it's not about "right" or "wrong," but just about what is memorable to an individual.

1930

1. Uruguay beat Argentina 4-2 to win the first World Cup in the sport of _____.
2. Mahatma Gandhi completed his march across India to protest the British tax on this basic spice: _____.
3. Astronomer Clyde Tombaugh discovered the dwarf planet _____.
4. Hostess marketed its mini sponge cake with a cream filling, "_____."
5. This year marked the release of antiwar film "All Quiet on the Western _____."
6. Ocean Spray Company introduced its flavorful juice made from _____.
7. July 7 marked the death of Sir Arthur Conan Doyle, creator of iconic detective Sherlock _____.
8. This cartoon character who resembled the "flapper" style of the 20s made her debut: Betty _____.
9. Mars introduced a new candy bar, topped with caramel and peanuts and covered with chocolate, "_____."
10. The first flight attendant, Helen Church, started work for this airline: _____.

ANSWERS TO 1930

1... Soccer
2... Salt
3... Pluto
4... Twinkie
5... Front
6... Cranberries
7... Holmes
8... Boop
9... Snickers
10... United

1931

1. This tallest building in the world opened in New York City: _____.
2. The "Star Spangled Banner" was approved by Hoover and Congress as our national _____.
3. Miles Lab introduced a drug combining aspirin with bi-carbonate of soda to settle the stomach, "Alka _____."
4. Construction began on a Colorado River project to generate power, the Hoover _____.
5. General Mills sold a new baking product, with pre-mixed flour, shortening, salt and baking powder, "_____."
6. The classic horror film about bewildered monster Frankenstein opened, starring Boris _____.
7. The George Washington Bridge opened, connecting New Jersey and _____.
8. Pearl S. Buck published her Pulitzer Prize-winning book, "The Good _____."
9. Connecticut manufacturer Schick began producing electric _____.
10. The state of Nevada legalized _____.

ANSWERS TO 1931

1... Empire State Building
2... Anthem
3... Seltzer
4... Dam
5... Bisquick
6... Karloff
7... New York
8... Earth
9... Razors
10... Gambling

1932

1. President Roosevelt's promise of reform to help people rise out of poverty was called "The New _____."
2. Sydney Harbour Bridge, the world's longest single-span bridge, opened in _____.
3. The Revenue Act instituted the first tax on gasoline at 1 cent per _____.
4. In an effort to provide jobs to more unemployed citizens, employers began reducing working _____.
5. The first non-stop solo flight across the Atlantic by a woman was made by Amelia _____.
6. World-famous aviator Charles Lindbergh paid a $50,000 ransom when his son was _____.
7. This murderous outlaw couple teamed up and began their life of crime: Bonnie and _____.
8. New York City's Rockefeller Center hailed the opening of this music hall: Radio _____.
9. Aldous Huxley authored his vision of the future in his novel, "A Brave New _____."
10. The "Tarzan the Ape Man" movie was a big hit, starring Johnny _____.

ANSWERS TO 1932

1... Deal
2... Australia
3... Gallon
4... Hours
5... Earhart
6... Kidnapped
7... Clyde
8... City
9... World
10... Weissmuller

1933

1. Newly-elected President Roosevelt inspired the US with his famous words, "The only thing we have to fear is _____."
2. The 21st Amendment to the Constitution ended the "noble experiment," otherwise known as _____.
3. Inventor Guy Tinkham came up with a flexible metal tray for use in a freezer to make _____.
4. Hitler was appointed Chancellor of _____.
5. A giant gorilla was the star of this film with the latest in special-effects: "King _____."
6. Motorists parked their cars in Camden, New Jersey to watch the first drive-in _____.
7. Scottish news reported this enormous creature seen rolling on the surface of a lake: Loch Ness _____.
8. In an effort to span the mile-wide strait that connects San Francisco Bay to the Pacific Ocean, work began on the Golden _____.
9. Farmers in the Great Plains states were plagued by devastating droughts and _____.
10. President Roosevelt began his series of informal radio addresses known as "Fireside _____."

ANSWERS TO 1933

1... Fear Itself
2... Prohibition
3... Ice Cubes
4... Germany
5... Kong
6... Movie
7... Monster
8... Gate Bridge
9... Dust Storms
10... Chats

1934

1. British author P.L. Travers published her novel about a perfect magical nanny, entitled "Mary _____."
2. Close to a million Americans fled from the Dust Bowl to the West coast seeking a better life; they were often called "_____."
3. A musical, "Anything Goes," about adventures on a luxury ocean liner, opened on _____.
4. This federal penitentiary opened on a rock island in the middle of San Francisco Bay: _____.
5. The National Biscuit Company (now Nabisco) introduced round, scalloped edged, snack crackers, "_____."
6. This Canadian couple became the proud parents of the first quintuplets to survive birth: _____.
7. This aquatic character made his debut in the cartoon "The Little Wise Hen:" Donald _____.
8. Woodstock, Vermont saw the opening of the first ski _____.
9. This famous childhood star appeared in her first movie, "Stand Up And Cheer:" Shirley _____.
10. A DuPont Chemicals laboratory produced the first successful synthetic fiber, _____.

ANSWERS TO 1934

1... Poppins
2... Okies
3... Broadway
4... Alcatraz
5... Ritz
6... The Dionnes
7... Duck
8... Tow (Rope)
9... Temple
10... Nylon

1935

1. An underground rail system with many beautiful, ornate stations opened in the Russian city of _____.
2. This Loony Tunes character made his debut: Porky _____.
3. An international foundation was founded to help members achieve sobriety, Alcoholics _____.
4. The Krueger Brewing Company in New Jersey introduced this alcoholic beverage in a can: _____.
5. A popular board game, based on buying property, houses and hotels, went on sale for $2.50, "_____."
6. Old-age pensions and unemployment insurance were provided to Americans with the passage of the Social _____.
7. This federal agency was created to put Americans back to work: the "Works Progress _____." ("WPA")
8. Gershwin's opera told the tragic story of two African-American lovers, Porgy and _____.
9. Babe Ruth retired with a 714 home run record not to be broken until 1974 by Hank _____.
10. Penguin Books in the UK produced the first-ever, easy to carry _____.

ANSWERS TO 1935

1... Moscow
2... Pig
3... Anonymous
4... Beer
5... Monopoly
6... Security Act
7... Administration
8... Bess
9... Aaron
10... Paperback Novel

1936

1. At the Berlin Summer Olympics four gold medals were won in track and field events by Jesse _____.
2. The first roadside stand in Georgia to sell homegrown pecans and candy was _____.
3. General Franco led an armed uprising of Nationalists against the Republic and started the Spanish _____.
4. To help market their dairy products, Borden Company created a cartoon of a female cow named _____.
5. The Oscar Mayer Company invented a vehicle to sell its product in the shape of a giant _____.
6. This new photo magazine was launched in the US, featuring news and human interest stories: "_____."
7. One of the year's biggest hit songs was "Pennies from Heaven" by Bing _____.
8. One way to beat the summer heat in NYC was to head to the seaside amusement area, Coney _____.
9. The Hoover Dam opened between Nevada and Arizona on this river: _____.
10. This 16-year-old was proclaimed king of Egypt when King Fuad died: _____.

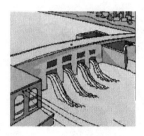

ANSWERS TO 1936

1... Owens
2... Stuckey's
3... Civil War
4... Elsie
5... Hot Dog
6... Life
7... Crosby
8... Island
9... Colorado
10... Farouk

1937

1. May 12th marked the coronation in Westminster Abbey of King George VI and Queen _____.
2. A&P supermarket expanded this magazine featuring food, cooking and home décor: "Woman's _____."
3. On July 2nd, this famous pioneering female aviator disappeared: Amelia _____.
4. After its flight across the Atlantic, this German dirigible exploded over New Jersey: _____
5. A commercial bakery was established, known for its breads, cookies and Goldfish crackers," Pepperidge _____."
6. One of Disney's most famous feature-length animated films was released, "Snow White and The _____."
7. Candy maker Mars produced a new chocolate bar with nougat of 3 different flavors, the "Three _____."
8. The world heavyweight-boxing championship was won by Joe _____.
9. Tolkien published this fantasy novel now thought to be a precursor to "Lord of the Rings:" "The _____."
10. Future President Ronald Reagan made his acting debut in the film "Love Is On The _____."

ANSWERS TO 1937

1... Elizabeth
2... Day
3... Earhart
4... Hindenburg
5... Farm
6... Seven Dwarves
7... Musketeers
8... Louis
9... Hobbit
10... Air

1938

1. Chester Carlson invented this new and easy way to make photocopies of paper: _____.
2. This multi-millionaire set a record by flying around the world in 3 days, 19 hours: Howard _____.
3. Orson Welles broadcast his sensational science fiction thriller, "The War of the _____."
4. Warner Brothers released its film starring Errol Flynn as the hero of Sherwood Forest, Robin _____.
5. Kate Smith sang a rendition of this Irving Berlin song for the first time on radio: "God Bless _____."
6. The health and safety of young people at work were protected with new federal laws called, "Child _____."
7. A dental hygiene product with long-lasting nylon bristles was invented, a _____.
8. The record for the fastest passenger liner to cross the Atlantic was beaten by The Queen _____.
9. To help combat polio, Roosevelt started a charitable foundation later known as The March of _____.
10. A device called the "Drunkometer" was first used to test a driver's level of drinking _____.

ANSWERS TO 1938

1... Xerox Copying
2... Hughes
3... Worlds
4... Hood
5... America
6... Labor Laws
7... Toothbrush
8... Mary
9... Dimes
10... Alcohol

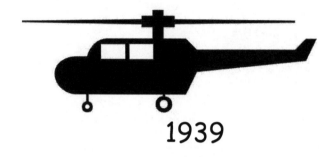

1939

1. A patent was issued for a disposable aerosol container for this dessert topping: whipped _____.
2. A star player for the Yankees was forced to retire after contracting a fatal disease called _____.
3. Igor Sikorsky developed America's first successful _____.
4. Vivien Leigh starred as Scarlett O'Hara in the film based on Mitchell's novel "Gone With The _____."
5. In the late 30s and early 40s this broadcaster's deep voice was heard on nightly radio: Edward R. _____.
6. On April 30th, Roosevelt opened this New York exhibition of wonders from around the world: _____.
7. Albert Einstein wrote a letter to the President warning about the possibility of an atomic _____.
8. The swinging tune "In the Mood" established this band as one of the country's most popular: Glenn _____.
9. Swiss company "Nestle" launched a quick breakfast drink that soon became a huge hit with the public, "Nescafe _____."
10. General Electric produced the first refrigerator with this added feature: _____.

ANSWERS TO 1939

1... Cream
2... Amyotrophic Lateral
    Sclerosis
.....(Lou Gehrig's Disease)
3... Helicopter
4... Wind
5... Murrow
6... The World's Fair
7... Bomb
8... Miller Band
9... Instant Coffee
10... A Freezer Compartment

LET'S PREVIEW THE 40s

The 1940s began with the horrific devastation of World War II, and then, fortunately, ended with prosperity. The first half of the decade saw Hitler's advances in Europe and the Japanese attack on Pearl Harbor. During the early 40's, citizens witnessed food shortages and rationing, "Scrap Drives," "Victory Gardens" and women working in factories. Following the war, Americans realized dreams of purchasing their own homes and having babies (the "Baby Boom"). As the atomic age began, so also did the "Cold War." As in previous times, music and entertainment were key aspects of everyday life. Big Bands continued to captivate, along with solo singers, bebop, rhythm and blues.

This decade's developments evoke a wide range of feelings: from sadness and anger over war-related events, to pride and joy with progress at home. Some readers will recall war stories shared by loved ones. Again, the aim of "Joggin" is to enjoy reliving the past while keeping feelings as positive as possible.

Can you connect with the introduction of the bikini and nylon stockings, novel candies like

"M&M's" and "Turkish Taffy;" toys like the "Erector Set" or "Slinky;" or the opening of national monuments like Mount Rushmore and the Lincoln Memorial? Personalize with questions about clothing, like: "Do you remember your first bathing suit? Where did you wear it? Who was with you? When you did get your first nylon stockings? Do you remember girdles and garter belts?" Or think about candy: "What was your favorite childhood candy? Did you shop at a neighborhood candy store? When did your parents treat you to candy? Do you remember candy associated with specific holidays or family gatherings?" Recall childhood games: "What was your favorite toy or game? Indoor game? Outdoor game? Game(s) played at family parties? Games played at school ... indoor or outdoor recess? Best game ever received as a gift? Did you ever make up your own games?" And facts about national monuments may conjure up memories of family trips--recall the places, people, times, feelings, sounds, tastes—whatever pops up! Enjoy!

1940

1. Hattie McDaniel was the first black person to win an Academy Award for her supporting role in "Gone With The _____."
2. Britain lost many men and ships when retreating from a powerful German advance on this French port: _____.
3. In US cafes, customers heard their favorite song by placing a coin in the slot of a _____.
4. Disney released this 2nd full-length film featuring an Italian woodcarver named Geppetto: "_____."
5. Roosevelt signed the Selective Service Act establishing the first peacetime _____.
6. Four French schoolboys out hunting rabbits discovered a cave full of prehistoric _____.
7. Women instantly loved this new legwear made with nylon fabric: _____.
8. July 7th marked the birth of famed "Beatles" drummer, Ringo _____.
9. A 5-year-old became the 14th spiritual leader of Tibetan Buddhists: The Dalai _____
10. A new candy was invented, little round chocolates with a letter "m" on one side, "_____."

ANSWERS TO 1940

1... Wind
2... Dunkirk
3... Jukebox
4... Pinocchio
5... Draft
6... Paintings
7... Stockings
8... Starr
9... Lama
10... M&M's

1941

1. Viewers saw the premier of Disney's animated film about a flying elephant, "_____."
2. Japanese naval and air forces bombed U.S. military bases at Pearl _____.
3. October 3rd marked the birth of a famous rock 'n' roll star who later introduced "The Twist," Chubby _____.
4. Britain destroyed what had been claimed to be Germany's unsinkable warship, the _____.
5. Electric taxis appeared in Paris to combat the shortage of _____.
6. Sculptures of four presidents were completed in the Black Hills of South Dakota on the face of Mount _____.
7. General Mills introduced a disc-shaped cereal, first advertised as oats, later as honey nuts, "_____."
8. During the war, blockades all over Europe and the rest of the word resulted in major food _____.
9. Wartime families around the world relied on this for news and entertainment: _____.
10. Orson Welles produced a film about an arrogant, power-hungry newspaper publisher, "Citizen _____."

ANSWERS TO 1941

1... Dumbo

2... Harbor

3... Checker

4... Bismarck

5... Gasoline

6... Rushmore

7... Cheerios

8... Shortages

9... Radio

10... Kane

1942

1. Women and children supported the war effort by collecting recyclables in "Scrap _____."
2. The Department of Agriculture encouraged Americans to plant vegetables in "Victory _____."
3. The Texas State Fair sold sausage on a stick, covered with fried corn batter and called a "corn _____."
4. At the University of Chicago physicist Enrico Fermi and his associates built the first atomic _____.
5. The Office of Price Administration began controlling the distribution of scarce goods through _____.
6. The symbol of the American women working in factories to support the war was Rosie the _____.
7. Command of all U.S. forces in Europe was given to Major General Dwight D. _____.
8. Bing Crosby released one of the most popular holiday songs of all time, "White _____."
9. This singing sensation debuted in NYC and eventually became one of the U.S.'s most popular crooners: Frank _____.
10. Glenn Miller won a gold record for his "Chattanooga _____."

ANSWERS TO 1942

1... Drives
2... Gardens
3... Dog
4... Reactor
5... Rationing
6... Riveter
7... Eisenhower
8... Christmas
9... Sinatra
10... Choo Choo

1943

1. This classic, award-winning film about a romance in Morocco during WWII was released: "_____."
2. Congress authorized this military unit comprised of women who joined the Army: _____.
3. For the first time, money was withheld from US workers' paychecks for income _____.
4. Roosevelt felt that the "beginning of the end" was the German defeat on the Italian island of _____.
5. New Yorkers flocked to Broadway to see this famous musical about life in America's heartland: "_____."
6. The opening number by Curly, the cowboy-hero in "Oklahoma," was "Oh What A _____."
7. The headquarters of the US War Department was dedicated in Virginia and known as the _____.
8. This future president's PT-109 was sunk by a Japanese destroyer: _____.
9. January 5 marked the death of a Tuskegee Institute professor, famous botanist and inventor, George Washington _____.
10. This memorial in Washington, DC was completed to honor the third president of the US: _____.

THOMAS JEFERSON

ANSWERS TO 1943

1... Casablanca
2... Women's Army Corps (WAC)
3... Tax
4... Sicily
5... Oklahoma
6... Beautiful Morning
7... Pentagon
8... John F. Kennedy
9... Carver
10... Jefferson Memorial

1944

1. On June 6, D-Day, Allied forces landed in France on the beaches of _____.
2. The United Fruit Company came out with an advertising jingle to help sell a product, called "Chiquita _____."
3. President Roosevelt signed legislation to help servicemen re-enter civilian life, called the GI _____.
4. This toy construction set with metal beams, nuts and bolts, continued to be a popular hit: _____.
5. Franklin D. Roosevelt became the only US president to be elected to a fourth _____.
6. New Yorkers were surprised by this very powerful and destructive 5.8 magnitude _____.
7. Benjamin Green invented a product to protect soldiers from the sun, _____.
8. January 12 marked the birth of this heavyweight champion who rivaled Muhammad Ali: Joe _____.
9. The family of this Jewish girl famous for her diary of the Holocaust was sent to concentration camps: _____.
10. The Education Act in Britain lifted the ban on women teachers' ability to _____.

ANSWERS TO 1944

1... Normandy
2... Banana
3... Bill
4... Erector Set
5... Term
6... Earthquake
7... Sunscreen
8... Frazier
9... Anne Frank
10... Marry

1945

1. The city of Paris reopened its famous art museum, the _____.
2. Grand Rapids, MI became the first city to fluoridate its _____.
3. This multi-national organization dedicated to peace and human rights held its first meeting: United _____.
4. Researchers developed "ENIAC," a most powerful calculating device considered to be the first _____.
5. Gimbel's Department Store demonstrated a toy that could travel down a flight of stairs, "_____."
6. The decision to drop two atomic bombs on Japanese cities was made by President Harry S. _____.
7. May 7th marked the end of the war in Europe, otherwise known as "_____."
8. US Navy Flight 19, a squadron of 5 torpedo bombers, disappeared over the Bermuda _____.
9. Gimbel's Department Store in NYC sold the first commercially made ballpoint _____.
10. One of the year's popular films was a musical comedy about two sailors on a leave in LA, "Anchors _____."

ANSWERS TO 1945

1... Louvre
2... Water
3... Nations
4... Computer
5... Slinky
6... Truman
7... V-E Day
8... Triangle
9... Pens
10... Aweigh

1946

1. This aircraft lifted by rotating blades became the first of its type certified for civilian use: _____.
2. Just in time for the "Baby Boom," "The Common Sense Book of Baby and Child Care" was written by _____.
3. "French's" food company introduced the first instant mashed _____.
4. A new plan by Britain and the US proposed to divide this land into Jewish and Arab states: _____.
5. A new swimsuit appeared in Paris, very tiny and in two pieces, called the _____.
6. Winston Churchill gave a famous speech in Fulton, MO, condemning the Soviet Union and its "Iron _____."
7. This international fund was created to provide help to children in war-torn or troubled countries: _____.
8. Berrill and Ware in England started a club meant to bring fun to those with very high IQs, _____.
9. The first festival to preview and judge international film making was held in _____.
10. Frances Xavier Cabrini, also called Mother Cabrini, was the first naturalized citizen of the US to be _____.

ANSWERS TO 1946

1... Helicopter
2... Dr. Spock
3... Potatoes
4... Palestine
5... Bikini
6... Curtain
7... UNICEF
8... Mensa
9... Cannes
10... Canonized

1947

1. Princess Elizabeth and Philip, Duke of Edinburgh, were married in London's Westminster _____.
2. A children's TV show featured Buffalo Bob Smith and his freckle-faced boy puppet Howdy _____.
3. Looney Tunes feline character Sylvester had fun chasing a yellow canary named _____.
4. An "instant" camera that developed its own pictures was developed by _____.
5. A talented athlete became the first African-American to play major league baseball, Jackie _____.
6. A "New Look" in women's fashion, with elegant designs, was unveiled by Frenchman Christian _____.
7. An archeological discovery was made when a herdsman in Palestine found jars filled with Dead Sea _____.
8. Daredevil pilot Chuck Yeager flew his bullet-shaped rocket plane faster than the speed of _____.
9. The classic, comedy-drama Christmas film opened, about a department store Santa, "Miracle On _____."
10. A charity was started by marines to distribute Christmas toys to needy kids, "Toys for _____."

ANSWERS TO 1947

1... Abbey
2... Doody
3... Tweety
4... Polaroid Corporation
5... Robinson
6... Dior
7... Scrolls
8... Sound
9... 34ᵗʰ Street
10... Tots

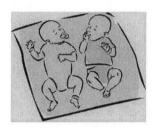

1948

1. President Truman signed an executive order that put an end to segregation in the US _____.
2. One of TV's greatest programs aired, an hour-long variety show seen on Sunday nights, the "Ed _____."
3. Home parties became a successful marketing strategy for plastic, airtight food containers called "_____."
4. The birthrate in the US continued to increase during the period that was to be known as the "Baby _____."
5. India witnessed the assassination of its strongest voice for peace and unity, Mahatma _____.
6. Columbia records released its first 12-inch record recognized for this technological advance: _____.
7. "Action paintings" with paint splashed over the canvas were developed by painters like Jackson _____.
8. A restaurant family made changes to their successful bar-b-que carhop to reopen it as the first _____.
9. This slap-stick comic superstar first appeared on TV every Tuesday night: Milton _____.
10. Norman Mailer published his famous war novel, "The Naked and the _____."

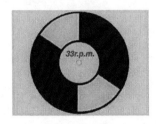

ANSWERS TO 1948

1... Military

2... Sullivan Show

3... Tupperware

4... Boom

5... Gandhi

6... Micro-groove,
   Long-playing

7... Pollock

8... McDonald's

9... Berle

10... Dead

1949

1. An Arthur Miller award-winning play about a tragic family man's story opened, "Death of a _____."
2. The Academy Award for Best Actor went to the British actor who played Hamlet, Laurence _____.
3. George Orwell published his acclaimed novel about a future totalitarian society, "_____."
4. The Academy of Television and Arts and Sciences presented its first _____.
5. RCA Victor produced a 7" record with a large center hole playing at the speed of _____.
6. "These Are My Children" was the first daytime melodrama, also called a "soap _____."
7. The Magic Clown TV show advertised a candy bar that would crack up and then melt in your mouth, "Turkish _____."
8. Housewives were thrilled with the advent of refrigerators offering freezers that were _____.
9. Cheerios sponsored a TV show about a masked Texan fighting for law and order, "The Lone _____."
10. This German-made "People's Car" was first sold in the US: _____.

ANSWERS TO 1949

1... Salesman
2... Olivier
3... 1984
4... Emmy Awards
5... 45 rpm
6... Opera
7... Taffy
8... Frost-free
9... Ranger
10... Volkswagen Beetle

LET'S PREVIEW THE 50s

When we think of the 50s, we can't help but think of Elvis Presley and Rock and Roll, and the influence of music and TV on American life. Teens sang and danced to the music of Bill Haley, Chuck Berry, Little Richard, and Jerry Lee Lewis, on jukeboxes and 45 rpm records and at "sock hops," or on "American Band Stand." TV entertained all ages: shows like "Mickey Mouse Club" and "Lassie" for children; soap operas for housewives; quiz shows, variety shows, comedies and late night talk shows for adults. The decade also saw the challenges of integration, civil rights and the cold war, as well as the impact of polio. As always, new books, comics, foods, toys, movies, Broadway shows, fashion and inventions added more enjoyment to everyday life.

As you review facts about the decade, you will find countless opportunities to reminisce. Talk about your favorite singers, songs and TV shows. Listen to old records or watch "You Tube" videos and sing or dance along if so inspired. A similar approach of accessing the internet or DVD's at the local library may also enhance memories of old movies and TV shows.

As always, try to personalize the information. For example, think about the introduction of the interstate highway system and how that changed family life. Talk about trips to visit relatives or while on vacation. Recall how long the drive took; what you did to pass the time; whether you stopped at "Howard Johnson's" or "McDonald's" restaurants; what your favorite snacks or meals were while on the road. Or maybe you packed food for the trip and stopped to picnic along the way? Did family members share the driving? Was anyone ever accused of being a "back seat driver?" Did you ever have car trouble, run out of gas or get stopped by the police? Did you ever get lost or have difficulty reading a map? How about getting caught in a bad storm or traffic jam? How did you find overnight lodging? Did you use the "AAA" travel guides? When and how did you learn to drive a car? You might enjoy comparing and contrasting automobile travel in the 50s vs. today!

1950

1. A new toy appeared, a bouncy, stretchy ball of goo sold in a plastic egg called "Silly _____."
2. Cartoonist Charles Schulz introduced the famous comic strip "_____."
3. This French master of contemporary art won the Venice Arts Festival grand prize: Henri _____.
4. A notable playwright of the 20th century passed away at his home in England, George Bernard _____.
5. The first credit cards launched in the US were called "Diner's _____."
6. Surgeon R.H. Lawler performed the first human transplant of this organ: _____.
7. This TV game show aired, in which panelists asked questions to guess the contestant's occupation: "What's My _____?"
8. Disney produced an animated musical fantasy film about a young woman with mean stepsisters, "_____."
9. This song about a sweetheart named Irene was one of the hottest of the year: "_____."
10. Kellogg's introduced a cereal that looked like puffed up balls of corn, "Corn _____."

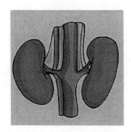

ANSWERS TO 1950

1... Putty
2... Peanuts
3... Matisse
4... Shaw
5... Club Cards
6... Kidney
7... Line
8... Cinderella
9... Goodnight Irene
10... Pops

1951

1. Swanson & Sons began selling their beef, chicken and turkey pot _____.
2. Among the first TV shows broadcast in color was Kukla, Fran and _____.
3. An American writer was born, who later took over her mother's newspaper advice column, "Hints from _____."
4. This show, starring Desi Arnaz and Lucille Ball, became TV's top-rated comedy: "I Love _____."
5. Engineers invented a new computer to handle alphabetic and numeric-characters called the _____.
6. New York's WCBS-TV broadcast its first baseball game shown in _____.
7. J.D. Salinger published his controversial book about a troubled teenager, "The Catcher In The _____."
8. A film about a complicated love triangle, with music from the Gershwin's, premiered in London: "An American In _____."
9. Disney released its animated film adaptation of the classic Lewis Carroll novel, "Alice In _____."
10. Popular song artists of the year included Perry Como, Mario Lanza and Nat King _____.

ANSWERS TO 1951

1... Pies

2... Ollie

3... Heloise

4... Lucy

5... UNIVAC

6... Color

7... Rye

8... Paris

9... Wonderland

10... Cole

1952

1. For the first time, movie audiences put on special glasses to watch films shot in _____.
2. Dr. Jonas Salk developed a vaccine to fight against _____.
3. When King George VI died, the new ruler of Britain became _____.
4. This restaurant chain opened its 351st location, with 28 flavors of ice cream: "Howard _____."
5. Teenager Maureen Connolly, nicknamed "Little Mo," competed at Wimbledon and won the title for _____.
6. For his brilliant medical work in Africa, this doctor was awarded the Nobel Peace Prize: Albert _____.
7. Amy Vanderbilt published her best-selling book, "Amy Vanderbilt's Complete Book of _____."
8. During the early 50s, many children watched movies like "Lassie the Dog" or "Roy Rogers" at Saturday _____.
9. The first toy to be advertised on TV, which required use of a real potato, was "Mr. _____."
10. Gene Kelly starred in one of Hollywood's most classic musical comedies, "Singing In The _____."

ANSWERS TO 1952

1... 3-D
2... Polio
3... Queen Elizabeth II
4... Johnson's
5... Women's Singles in Tennis
6... Schweitzer
7... Etiquette
8... Matinees
9... Potato Head
10... Rain

1953

1. Right around this time, women began wearing the latest daring footwear, _____.
2. Scientists discovered the structure responsible for our inherited characteristics, _____.
3. Two brave climbers reached the summit of the world's highest mountain, _____.
4. Ernest Hemmingway won a Pulitzer Prize for his classic novel "The Old Man and The _____."
5. Leather-clad Marlon Brando starred in this film about a motorcycle gang: "The Wild _____."
6. This famous couple was executed for spying against the US: Julius and Ethel _____.
7. The 34th President of the US, A WWII hero, was inaugurated, Dwight D. _____.
8. Hugh Heffner's "Playboy" magazine began, with the first issue featuring nude photos of Marilyn _____.
9. The Kraft food company introduced its processed cheese spread known as "Cheez _____."
10. Patti Page sang her rendition of a song that was No. 1 in US "Billboard Magazine" for 8 weeks, "How Much Is That _____."

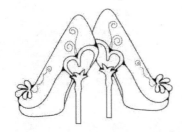

ANSWERS TO 1953

1... Spike Heeled Stilettoes
2... DNA
3... Mount Everest
4... Sea
5... One
6... Rosenberg
7... Eisenhower
8... Monroe
9... Whiz
10... Doggie in the Window?

1954

1. The period of heightened tension between the US and the Soviet Union was called the "_____."
2. Housewives were excited when General Electric began selling its first colored kitchen _____.
3. Frank Sinatra won an Oscar for his role in the film "From Here to _____."
4. This Mississippi "King of Rock and Roll" released his first single, "That's All Right Mama:" _____.
5. Construction began on one of the world's most famous theme parks, located in Anaheim California, _____.
6. The Brown v. Board of Education Supreme Court decision ruled against _____.
7. This top player in the world of golf won another Masters Golf Tournament: Sam _____.
8. President Eisenhower signed an order that added two words to the "Pledge of Allegiance," "_____."
9. The first volume of "Lord of the Rings" was published, written by J.R.R. _____.
10. Ford Motor Company released this classic sports car to compete with the Chevy Corvette: _____

ANSWERS TO 1954

1... Cold War

2... Appliances

3... Eternity

4... Elvis Presley

5... Disneyland

6... Segregation in Public Schools

7... Snead

8... Under God

9... Tolkien

10... Thunderbird

1955

1. This African-American woman made history when she refused to move from her bus seat: Rosa _____.
2. African-American Marian Anderson made history when she performed at the New York _____.
3. A popular toy putty, non-toxic, colorful, reusable and packaged in a can, was called "_____."
4. Children sang and danced as "Mouseketeers" on the newly released television program, the "_____."
5. Older folks watched "Marshal Matt Dillon," "Chester," and "Miss Kitty" on the Western series "_____."
6. A poster for this sexy actress showed her standing over a subway grating with her skirt flying: _____.
7. Ray Kroc opened the first of the world's largest restaurant franchises, known by its golden arches, "_____."
8. This famous 26-year-old actor, known for portraying a teenage rebel, was killed in a car crash: James_____.
9. Tennessee Williams was awarded the Pulitzer Prize for his work, "Cat on a _____."
10. The minimum hourly wage went from 75 cents to one _____.

ANSWERS TO 1955

1... Parks
2... Metropolitan Opera
3... Play Doh
4... Mickey Mouse Club
5... Gunsmoke
6... Marilyn Monroe
7... McDonald's
8... Dean
9... Hot Tin Roof
10... Dollar

1956

1. Charlton Heston traveled to Egypt to portray Moses in the Cecil B. DeMille film "Ten _____."
2. Movie actress Grace Kelly married Prince Rainier III of _____.
3. An Italian ocean liner collided shortly before its anticipated arrival in NYC, the Andrea _____.
4. Some 54 million watched Sullivan's "Toast of the Town" show to view 21-year-old rock-and-roller _____.
5. A French company marketed the first nonstick frying pan coated with _____.
6. Edina, Minnesota enjoyed the first ever, fully enclosed, climate-controlled shopping _____.
7. "And God Created Woman" was released, starring sensual and liberated actress Brigitte _____.
8. Yankee pitcher Don Larsen set a record in the World Series when he threw the first ever _____.
9. This heavyweight boxing champion retired at age 31, with a perfect record of 39 wins/fights: Rocky _____.
10. Federal legislation authorized the creation of an interstate system of _____.

ANSWERS TO 1956

1... Commandments
2... Monaco
3... Doria
4... Elvis Presley
5... Teflon
6... Mall
7... Bardot
8... Perfect Game
9... Marciano
10... Highways

1957

1. The President sent troops to Little Rock, Arkansas to enforce school _____.
2. The Soviet Union launched the first man-made space satellite, _____.
3. This romantic Broadway musical highlighted tensions between the "Jets" and the "Sharks": "_____."
4. Colonel Sanders began selling his Kentucky Fried Chicken in containers as large as _____.
5. A new "flying saucer" toy was released, controlled with a flick of the wrist and called a "_____."
6. A lighter ice chest to chill and transport beverages was invented, made out of _____.
7. Dr. Seuss wrote his new book with only 175 words written in comic verse, "The Cat In The _____."
8. Argentinian race car driver Fangio won his fifth world championship at the Grand _____.
9. Dick Clark's television show featured teenagers dancing to hit tunes on "American _____."
10. A committee of scientific heart and cancer experts reported a relationship between lung cancer and _____.

ANSWERS TO 1957

1... Integration
2... Sputnik
3... West Side Story
4... Buckets
5... Frisbee
6... Foam
7... Hat
8... Prix
9... Bandstand
10... Smoking

1958

1. The Roman Catholic Church elected one of the most popular popes of all time, _____.
2. The first nuclear-powered submarine, "USS Nautilus," became the first ship to reach the North _____.
3. This famous 23-year-old rock and roll singer and movie star was drafted into the army: _____.
4. Baseball fans in New York were sad to see the Brooklyn Dodgers and New York Giants move to _____.
5. A #1 song hit was "The Chipmunk Song," with Alvin, Simon and _____.
6. The US launched satellite "Explorer I' from its launch pad in Cape _____.
7. Men had to look "cool" while playing or listening to music, styling their hair with a little dab of "_____."
8. One of the latest toys sensations was a plastic hoop to twirl around the waist, called the "_____."
9. Thousands of babies were born with deformities due to this drug marketed for morning sickness: _____.
10. Another hugely popular toy was the plastic interlocking building block, "_____."

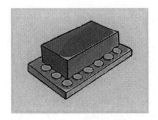

ANSWERS TO 1958

1... Pope John XXIII
2... Pole
3... Elvis Presley
4... California
5... Theodore
6... Canaveral, Florida
7... Brylcreem
8... Hula Hoop
9... Thalidomide
10... Lego

1959

1. The US admitted its 49th and 50th states, _____.
2. Fans were stunned when a plane crash killed 3 rock and roll stars, Valens, the "Big Bopper" and Buddy _____.
3. Revolutionaries overtook the government in Cuba, led by the rebel commander, Fidel _____.
4. America's TV audience was shocked by the revelation of the rigging of winnings on _____.
5. The world witnessed the completion of a waterway connecting the Great Lakes and the Atlantic Ocean, the St. Lawrence _____.
6. Mattel toys manufactured a glamorous doll who has raised considerable controversy over time, "_____."
7. This Colorado brewery became the first to use an all-aluminum beer can: _____.
8. This blockbuster biblical film, famous for Charlton Heston's chariot race, was released: "_____."
9. A Rodgers and Hammerstein musical opened on Broadway, about the von Trapp family's story: "The Sound of _____."
10. The Recording Academy began recognizing achievement in the music industry by awarding _____.

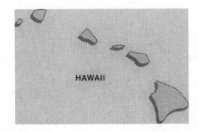

HAWAII

ANSWERS TO 1959

1... Alaska and Hawaii
2... Holly
3... Castro
4... Quiz Shows
5... Seaway
6... Barbie
7... Coors
8... Ben Hur
9... Music
10... Grammy Awards

LET'S PREVIEW THE 60s

Social and political turmoil dominated the scene in the 1960s. Civil rights and antiwar protests were slow to bring about change, and unrest was manifested in the assassinations of John F. Kennedy, Martin Luther King, Jr., and then Robert F. Kennedy. Also in the anti-establishment lifestyle of the hippies; draft dodgers; and lyrics of Bob Dylan, Joan Baez and others. The "Cold War" continued, as well as confrontation at the Bay of Pigs and Berlin Wall. In the meantime, more positive developments centered on space exploration, with Russian and American scientists racing to land a man on the moon. And as always, countless talented inventors, authors, actors, artists, playwrights and musicians enhanced the everyday lives of Americans.

Here are a few final tips as your proceed through this last decade. Many will connect with the music of the Beatles, their first appearance on TV and screaming fans in the audience. Recall your collection of 33 rpm record albums, when you most frequently listened, attended concerts or parties. You might have trekked to Woodstock or visited San Francisco. Challenge yourself to recall the dances of the day: the Twist, Stroll, Frug, Dog, Mashed Potato, Madison, Hully Gully, Watusi, Pony, Hitch Hike.

As a young man, did you let your hair grow-- maybe even into a ponytail; wear grungy jeans, bell bottoms, leather vests and beads? As a young woman, did you wear peasant blouses, tie-dyes, long, messy hair, mini or maxi skirts? Recall parents' reactions when their children shopped at Army surplus stores, went bra-less, or marched in civil rights or anti-war protests. Or campus officials and police responding to pot-smoking students. Men might recall their experience with the military ... their draft number, whether they or friends were drafted, what some did to avoid the draft, military experiences and understanding of the Vietnam War. And almost all Americans can clearly remember the exact moment they learned of the assassination of President John F. Kennedy.

Individual "fill-in the blank" items will jog readers' memories, but more enjoyment may result from reliving personal experiences.

1960

1. Alfred Hitchcock terrified viewers with the gruesome murder of a young woman as she showered in "_____."
2. Barefooted African athlete Abebe Bikila made history when he won an Olympic gold medal in _____.
3. Wilma Rudolph won Olympic gold despite having been a victim of the crippling childhood disease _____.
4. Over 50 victims were gunned down when protesting South Africa's racial policy known as _____.
5. This animated sitcom series debuted, depicting Barney Rubble and others in everyday life among cavemen in the town of Bedrock: "The _____."
6. African Americans protested segregation at lunch counters and other places by staging "_____."
7. During the "Cold War," Americans tried to protect against nuclear attack by building fallout _____.
8. American pilot Francis Gary Powers was shot down and tried as a spy by _____.
9. For the first time television allowed American voters to observe the presidential candidates in a _____.
10. Chubby Checker introduced this dance craze: _____.

ANSWERS TO 1960

1... Psycho
2... The Marathon
3... Polio
4... Apartheid
5... Flintstones
6... Sit-ins
7... Shelters
8... The Soviet Union
9... Debate
10... The Twist

1961

1. Twenty-seven-year-old Russian cosmonaut Yuri Gagarin became the first man in _____.
2. About 1400 Cuban exiles attempted an invasion of Cuba when they landed at the Bay of _____.
3. Americans trained and volunteered to spend 2 years in service to other countries under this program: The Peace _____.
4. East Germany closed off the route into the West by constructing the Berlin _____.
5. A lemon-lime flavored, carbonated drink was introduced to compete with "7-Up," "_____."
6. Babe Ruth's record for homers in one season was beaten by Yankees' slugger Roger _____.
7. This famous singer-songwriter, known for social and political lyrics, signed with Columbia Records: Bob _____.
8. The first disposable diaper was introduced by _____.
9. A newly released television sitcom featured a talking horse named "Mr. _____."
10. One of ballet's most talented male dancers defected from Russia, Rudolf _____.

ANSWERS TO 1961

1... Space
2... Pigs
3... Corps
4... Wall
5... Sprite
6... Maris
7... Dylan
8... Pampers
9... Ed
10... Nureyev

1962

1. US spaceship "Friendship 7" orbited the earth, piloted by astronaut John _____.
2. This hairstyle for men, cut very short and used in the military, lessened in popularity: _____
3. "Pop art" emerged, with masterpieces like Andy Warhol's famous images of Campbell's _____.
4. At age 11, this famous blind singer-songwriter signed with Motown records: Stevie _____.
5. Rachel Carson published her classic book about the ill effects of chemicals on the environment, "Silent _____."
6. James Bond made his film debut in "Dr. No," played by actor Sean _____.
7. The Nobel Prize in literature was awarded to John Steinbeck, for his work, "Of Mice and _____."
8. Gregory Peck starred in a classic film about racism in the US, "To Kill A _____."
9. An observation tower was built for the World's Fair in Seattle, WA and called the "Space _____."
10. Marvel Comics introduced this superhero with clinging powers and "web shooters": "_____."

ANSWERS TO 1962

1... Glenn
2... Crew Cut
3... Soup Cans
4... Wonder
5... Spring
6... Connery
7... Men
8... Mockingbird
9... Needle
10... Spiderman

1963

1. The most significant event of the year for US citizens was the assassination of _____.
2. The US Postal Service introduced a new system of codes to improve mail delivery called _____.
3. The Lacoste Company in France patented a tennis racket made of _____.
4. Britain's Profumo resigned when charged with having sex with Soviet-involved prostitute Christine _____.
5. Martin Luther King inspired the largest civil rights crowd ever with his words "I have a _____."
6. At the age of 26, Tereshkova from the Soviet Union became the first woman to go into _____.
7. Children's author M. Sendak published his brilliantly illustrated classic, "Where the Wild _____."
8. On June 12th, Medgar Evers was assassinated, a chief civil rights leader in Mississippi for the National Association for the Advancement of _____.
9. Beatles released their hit, "I Want to Hold _____."
10. The most expensive film to date was released, an epic drama about a young Queen of Eqypt, "_____."

ANSWERS TO 1963

1... President J.F. Kennedy
2... Zip Codes
3... Steel
4... Keeler
5... Dream
6... Space
7... Things Are
8... Colored People
9... Your Hand
10... Cleopatra

1964

1. This leader of the Soviet Union was ousted: Nikita _____.

2. President Johnson signed historical legislation outlawing racial discrimination, the "Civil _____."

3. This group of female singers began recording with the label Motown: Diana Ross and the _____.

4. The leader of S. Africa's movement opposing apartheid was sentenced to life in prison, Nelson _____.

5. Black actor Sydney Poitier won an Oscar for his outstanding performance in "Lilies of the _____."

6. This hottest rock group from England appeared on the "Ed Sullivan Show": _____.

7. Three young men volunteering for the "Freedom Summer Project" were murdered by Ku Klux _____.

8. After meeting on the set of "Cleopatra," screen star Elizabeth Taylor married Richard _____.

9. World heavyweight champion title went from Sonny Liston to Cassius _____.

10. Roald Dahl published his children's novel about a boy's adventures in "Charlie and the Chocolate _____."

ANSWERS TO 1964

1... Khrushchev
2... Rights Act
3... Supremes
4... Mandela
5... Field
6... The Beatles
7... Klan
8... Burton
9... Clay
10... Factory

1965

1. Racial riots erupted with fires, shooting and looting in a section of Los Angeles known as _____.
2. Customers loved redeeming these stamps earned at many stores for products in a catalog: "S& H _____."
3. The first covered baseball stadium was completed in Texas, known as the Houston _____.
4. The last link in this monument built in the shape of an arch was placed in St. Louis, MO: _____.
5. On November 9th, at the height of rush hour, a short circuit caused darkness across the Northeast in an event remembered as the "Great _____."
6. Ed White, onboard *Gemini 4*, became the first American to perform this feat in outer space: _____.
7. U of Florida football team, the "Gators" tried a new drink purported to replace electrolytes, "_____."
8. Walt Disney's *Mary Poppins* won five Oscars in Hollywood, with this lead actress: Julie _____.
9. One of the most popular daytime soap operas debuted in November, "Days of Our _____."
10. An epic film premiered, about two lovers separated during the Russian Revolution, "Dr. _____."

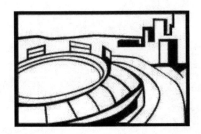

ANSWERS TO 1965

1... Watts
2... Green Stamps
3... Astrodome
4... Gateway Arch
5... Blackout
6... Walk
7... Gatorade
8... Andrews
9... Lives
10... Zhivago

1966

1. Women's fashion saw hems climbing upwards toward the upper thigh in skirts called _____.
2. The film version of "The Sound of Music," left movie fans singing songs like "Do-Re- _____."
3. The Supreme Court's "Miranda Decision" gave arrested citizens the "right to remain _____."
4. India elected a new 48-year-old woman prime minister, Indira _____.
5. The unmanned spaceship "Surveyor" became the first to land on the _____.
6. Under a new ruling by the Vatican, Catholics were no long required to abstain from meat on _____.
7. This science-fiction TV series began, with Capt. Kirk, Mr. Spock and the "Enterprise" crew on "Star_____."
8. A former TV star was elected governor of California, Ronald _____.
9. Simon and Garfunkel released their album "Sounds of _____."
10. December 15th marked the death of animated film and amusement park industries icon, Walt _____.

ANSWERS TO 1966

1... Miniskirts
2... Mi
3... Silent
4... Gandhi
5... Moon
6... Fridays
7... Trek
8... Reagan
9... Silence
10... Disney

1967

1. Federal law required packaging to disclose ingredients, place of business and weight of _____.
2. A female folk singer and anti-Vietnam war activist was arrested at a protest in CA, Joan _____.
3. Fans were thrilled to watch Green Bay Packers beat Kansas City Chiefs in the first football Super _____.
4. Fire aboard "Apollo 1" killed three astronauts, Edward White, Roger Chaffee, and Virgil (Gus) _____.
5. In South Africa, Dr. Christian Barnard performed the first successful heart _____.
6. Award-winning film "The Graduate" was released, with Anne Bancroft, Katharine Ross, and Dustin _____.
7. Heavyweight champion Cassius Clay, now Muhammad Ali, refused to be drafted due to his _____.
8. Thurgood Marshall became the first African American to be named to the U.S. Supreme _____.
9. An hour-long TV comedy and variety show with political satire debuted, "The Smothers _____.
10. Ralph Nader's book "Unsafe at Any Speed" prompted laws to improve safety standards for _____.

ANSWERS TO 1967

1... Food
2... Baez
3... Bowl
4... Grissom
5... Transplant
6... Hoffman
7... Religion
8... Court
9... Brothers
10... Cars

1968

1. The first of a new restaurant chain opened in Florida, billed as a seafood lover's haven, "The Red _____."
2. An hour-long weekly news show, reporting on corruption and key issues, first aired, "60 _____."
3. This nonviolent leader of the civil rights movement was murdered by a white supremacist: Martin _____.
4. Another assassination took the life of this young attorney while he was campaigning: Robert F. _____.
5. Widow Jackie Kennedy married a Greek business executive, Aristotle _____.
6. The "Students for a Democratic Society" continued to organize marches and protests against the _____.
7. Shirley Chisholm became the first black woman to be elected to the U.S. House of _____.
8. A controversial rock musical opened in London, with profanity, illegal drugs, and nudity, "_____."
9. The US instituted a phone number to call in case of an emergency, _____.
10. First Pennsylvania Bank introduced the first "ATM," or "automated teller _____."

ANSWERS TO 1968

1... Lobster
2... Minutes
3... Luther King, Jr.
4... Kennedy
5... Onassis
6... Vietnam War
7... Representatives
8... Hair
9... 911
10... Machine

1969

1. These 2 astronauts became the first men to walk on the moon: Edwin ("Buzz") Aldrin and Neil _____.
2. Some 400,000 young people came together in love and peace to enjoy a music festival at _____.
3. Long-haired folks, wearing tunics, beads and bell-bottoms, and often smoking pot, were called "_____."
4. Miniskirts were replaced by hemlines that reached down to the floor, called _____.
5. Kermit, Oscar, Big Bird, Bert and Ernie became part of an educational TV show for preschool kids, "_____."
6. American actress and singer, most known for her role as Dorothy in the "Wizard of Oz," died, Judy _____.
7. This British-French supersonic airliner made its first 28-minute flight: _____.
8. Earl Warren was succeeded as Chief Justice of the Supreme Court by Warren E. _____.
9. Film stars Paul Newman and Robert Redford teamed up as a pair of outlaws in "Butch Cassidy and the _____."
10. The ultimate American muscle car was released by Pontiac, the _____.

ANSWERS TO 1969

1... Armstrong
2... Woodstock
3... Hippies or Flower People
4... Maxi Skirts
5... Sesame Street
6... Garland
7... Concorde
8... Burger
9... Sundance Kid
10... Firebird

1970

1. Americans celebrated the first of an annual event to support environmental protection, called _____.
2. Ohio National Guardsmen were sent to this university to maintain order during an antiwar protest: _____.
3. 50,000 women paraded down 5th Avenue to support the women's liberation movement led by Betty _____.
4. The voting age in the US was lowered from 21 to

   _____.
5. The Beatles officially broke up when this member stated he was leaving: Paul _____.
6. The world's first commercial jumbo-jet flew from New York to London, a Boeing 747 operated by Pan-_____.
7. President Nixon proposed an agency to support health and the environment, the Environmental _____.
8. Orville Redenbacher and partner Charlie Bowman launched this snack product: _____.
9. For the first time, TV broadcast this live sports event every Monday night: _____.
10. General Mills introduced a boxed food consisting of dried pasta with seasonings to be cooked with ground beef and called "Hamburger _____."

ANSWERS TO 1970

1... Earth Day
2... Kent State
3... Friedan
4... 18
5... McCartney
6... Am
7... Protection Agency
8... Gourmet Popping Corn
9... Football
10... Helper

Made in the USA
San Bernardino, CA
06 March 2019